Autumn and Winter Nature Activities for Waldorf Kindergartens

Translated by Ronald E. Koetzsch

First published in German as *Natur-Kinder-Garten-Werkstatt: Herbst*
and *Natur-Kinder-Garten-Werkstatt: Winter* by Verlag Freies Geistesleben, Stuttgart
First published in English as *Autumn Nature Activities for Children* in 2005 and
Winter Nature Activities for Children in 2006 by Floris Books, Edinburgh
This combined edition 2021

© 2001 Verlag Freies Geistesleben & Urachhaus GmbH
Translation © 2005, 2021 Floris Books

All rights reserved. No part of this publication may
be reproduced without the prior permission of
Floris Books, Edinburgh
www.florisbooks.co.uk

British Library CIP Data available
ISBN 978-178250-667-6
Printed in Poland through Hussar

 Floris Books supports sustainable forest management by printing this book on materials made from wood that comes from responsible sources and reclaimed material

Autumn and Winter Nature Activities for Waldorf Kindergartens

Irmgard Kutsch ❀ Brigitte Walden

Floris Books

CONTENTS

Introduction   6

September
Healthy food   10
Harvesting and preparation   12
The Little Pot That Was Always Full   18

October
Basket-making   22
House-building   26

November
Caring for birds   34
Beeswax   38
Dipping candles   40
Making paper   42
Painting and handicrafts   46

December
Advent	52
An Advent Story	54
Christmas scenes	56

January
Working with wool	60
Weaving	66
Knitting	72
Felting	73
Magic wool	75

February
Willow hedge	78
Wooden toys	80
Carving Twigs in Kindergarten	86
More wood projects	88
Working with clay	90

Resources 94

INTRODUCTION

This is two-year-old Saskia. Like almost all children of this age, she has a deep interest in the natural world. She has worked tirelessly now for one hour, picking up apples from underneath the tree, bringing them one by one to the water bucket, and washing them. She has discovered to her surprise that, although she carefully dunks them again and again into the water, they never stay on the bottom but come stubbornly back to the top. This gives her great pleasure and inspires her to try again.

The newly fallen apples give off such a delicious aroma that Saskia takes a bite out of one. The sour taste is not very nice. Again and again, she takes an apple in both hands and, from a short distance, throws it into the water bucket where it lands with a dull splash among the other apples.

She totters with a hurried step over the bumpy ground of the garden, and her muscles and her sense of balance must work hard to stop her from falling down. Finally her socks and sweater have become so wet that, despite her loud protests, her mother calls Saskia away.

The variety of sensory perceptions and of opportunities for sense development in this scenario are significant. From this engrossing activity, Saskia has a fresh, healthy glow in her cheeks, and her hands and feet — despite the work in cold water — are snugly warm afterward. So much exercise in the fresh air brings a hearty appetite. Saskia sits down to eat, a little tired — as might be expected — and regains the energy she has exuberantly expended. Time for a nap in her cosy bed, where she falls into a deep sleep.

This scene is one of many that have shown me how important life in and with nature is for child development. I see this especially in my work in kindergartens and schools for children with special needs. Being outside in nature has a harmonising effect and children can start to learn about the interconnectedness of all things.

These books are to help educators who want to foster healthy child development through nature experiences in daycare centres, playgroups, early childhood programmes, kindergartens, and in work with children with disabilities. It offers situation-based and experience-based options for nature teaching. We have consciously avoided discussing teaching theory and hope that these activities will bring together open-minded people who are looking for a new direction, or new inspiration.

This book developed out of the everyday practice of the Children's Nature and Garden Centre in Reichshof, Germany.

In each activity, we introduce the children to different seasonal aspects of nature. In mixed-age kindergarten groups, the youngest children tend to explore materials in an unfocused, but very imaginative, way. Older children look for ways to do 'real' work. Both unfocused play and movement, and purposeful work, offer possibilities for developing practical intelligence. The key is to always have an appropriately busy adult for the children to imitate.

Irmgard Kutsch

SEPTEMBER

Pumpkins take a long time to grow. Now the children can enjoy jolly lanterns and delicious soup.

This sugar beet lantern was made at a harvest festival on a biodynamic farm.

Biodynamic farms

More and more farmers are recognising the damage to the environment of large-scale animal farming and monoculture. Increasing numbers of farms and gardens have converted to more natural methods of producing basic foods such as fruit, vegetables, eggs, milk and grains, including biodynamic farms.

The feed for animals raised on biodynamic farms is predominantly grown on the farm itself. The fertiliser for meadows, pasture land, and for grain and vegetable fields comes from carefully tended compost piles, which use manure from the animals on the farm and are allowed to mature over time. Thus a biodynamic farm is a self-contained agricultural organism.

These farms do not see themselves only as places of food production. They are concerned about caring for the earth and for the small and even microscopic organisms that inhabit it. This leads to a healthy and productive natural environment. The interplay of earth, water, air, light, and even the influence of the stars, is considered in all phases of the agricultural process from sowing to harvesting.

Children are often very interested to see how labour-intensive ecological farming is: work is mainly done by hand, rather than by machines.

HEALTHY FOOD

September is a month of abundance – ripe fruit and vegetables, and grain stores that are full to bursting. Our supermarkets are permanently full of produce, and we should be conscious of how far some foods have travelled, as well as how they are packaged.

In a Waldorf kindergarten, healthy vegetable- and fruit-based lunches and snacks are very important The preperation of food should be seen as an enriching educational activity.

Eating together

The preperation of healthy meals, eaten together, has been part of the Waldorf approach for decades. Here are some things to consider.

At festival times, the meal should reflect the meaning of the holiday and should be clearly something special. When there are children from ethnic minorities and from other countries in the kindergarten, it is important that their festivals are celebrated, and that food from their culture is included.

After we have thought about *what* to eat, we must consider *how* to eat it.

We recommend:

- eating together at one large table
- setting the table and decorating it together
- serving the meal that has been prepared together
- saying a grace or blessing the meal
- dividing up the work of clearing the table, washing up and putting things away

Repetition is powerful, and children will begin to sense that the beautiful sounds and rhymes bring a rich inner nourishment to open and expectant souls.

HARVESTING AND PREPARATION

When children are involved in harvesting and preparing vegetables and fruit, especially from their own garden, they experience in the best possible way the connectedness of human life and nature. Through the work itself, their senses are enriched and trained, and their motor skills are developed.

In the early autumn, we gather the harvest and work with it so that it will keep through the autumn and winter. The children are often delighted when, during the cold months, they find fruit that they harvested and processed months earlier reappearing on special occasions in yoghurt, muesli, birthday cake, as jam on bread or as a piece of dried fruit.

When children have all been involved in the preparation of the meal, it is nice to eat together at one table.

Working with their father, the children press fresh apples.

Clockwise from top left:

Because of their thorns, blackberries are plants that children will treat with great respect.

In kindergartens with limited space, these box-potatoes give children an opportunity to experience potatoes from planting the sprout right through to harvesting.

At a young age, children can take part in age-appropriate work in the kitchen.

When fruit is processed right after picking, children can experience the true flavour and aroma.

Recipes for harvested fruit

Baked apples

Use one large apple per person. Core the apples almost all the way through, leaving a little of the apple at the bottom to make a cavity. Fill the cavity with nuts, honey and cinnamon, and top with a pat of butter. Bake in a buttered pan with a little water for about 2 hours at 325 °F/150 °C or until the apples are tender. They taste particularly delicious baked on an open fire.

Jam from fresh fruit

1 ½ pounds (750 g) of fresh fruit
½ pound (250 ml) of honey
Add 1–3 teaspoons of pectin if needed for thickening

Mix washed, cut-up fruit with the honey and pectin and heat, stirring constantly, not over 110 °F/40 °C. Let it stand and thicken for about 10 minutes. Fill jars with the jam and put them in the refrigerator. The jam keeps for three to four weeks. To keep for longer, sterilise the jars and seal them.

Fruit juice from steamed fruit

10 pounds (5 kg) fruit
1 pound (500 g) sugar

Wash the fruit. Put it in the basket of a steamer and sprinkle with sugar. Fill the lower section with 1 quart (1 litre) of water. Cover and bring to the boil. Over a moderate heat the fruit yields its juice in about an hour. Pour the juice into warm, sterilised bottles and seal immediately.

Jelly from fruit juice

Mix 1 quart (1 l) of fruit juice and 2 pounds (1 kg) of granulated/preserving sugar in a heavy saucepan. Cook for four minutes at a rolling boil. Put in warm, dry, sterilised glasses and seal.

Jam for the winter larder

2 pounds (1 kg) fruit
1 ½ pounds (750 g) granulated/preserving sugar

Wash the fruit and remove seeds and stones. Cut into small pieces. Put into a large, shallow saucepan and slowly bring to the boil. Gradually add the sugar. Cook, stirring, for about thirty minutes until enough liquid has boiled off to thicken the jam. Test on a spoon for thickness and taste. Pour the hot jam into hot sterilised jars with screw tops.

Yoghurt herb salad dressing

1 pound (500 g) plain natural yoghurt
1 teaspoon salt
1 tablespoon sugar
juice of 2 lemons
mixed fresh herbs

Take a small amount of each of the herbs available in the garden: for example, three sprigs of parsley, ten chive stalks, a little cress and so on. Wild herbs, such as dandelion or stinging nettle, are also excellent. Finely cut the herbs. Mix all the ingredients in a large bowl and pour over a green salad. Garnish with slices of radish or parsley leaves.

Cake with seasonal fruit

½ pound (200 g) butter
4 ounces (100 g) sugar
lemon
oil
2 eggs
½ pound (200 g) fresh ground whole-wheat flour
2 teaspoons baking powder

(For 25 children, double the recipe)
Mix all the ingredients thoroughly and put the batter in a greased baking tin. Decorate the top with pieces of fruit. Bake for 45 minutes at 350 °F/180 °C.

Dried fruit

Core and slice apples and pears. Cut plums and apricots in half, removing the stones.

Put parchment/greaseproof baking paper on baking sheets; spread out the fruit slices in a single layer and let them dry slowly at 110–130 °F/40–50 °C in the oven or on a radiator. The fruit could also be cut into small pieces, strung on strong thread or twine and hung up to dry. Apple peel can be dried for tea.

Apple pancakes (serves 20)

To make the batter: mix together 1 pound (500 g) of fresh ground whole-wheat flour, four eggs, a quart (1 litre) of milk, and 2 teaspoons of salt.

Core 1 pound (500 g) of apples and cut into small pieces. Put a little oil in a hot frying pan, then a ladle of batter. Sprinkle with apple pieces. Flip the pancake after a few minutes to cook the other side.

The Apple

1. With-in a lit-tle ap-ple so co-sy and so small, there are five lit-tle cham-bers a-round a lit-tle hall.
2. In ev'ry room are sleep-ing two seeds of gold-en brown. They're ly-ing there and dream-ing in beds of ei-der-down.
3. They're dream-ing there of sun-shine and how it's going to be, when they shall hang as ap-ples up-on a Christ-mas tree.

Oats, Peas, Beans and Barley Grow

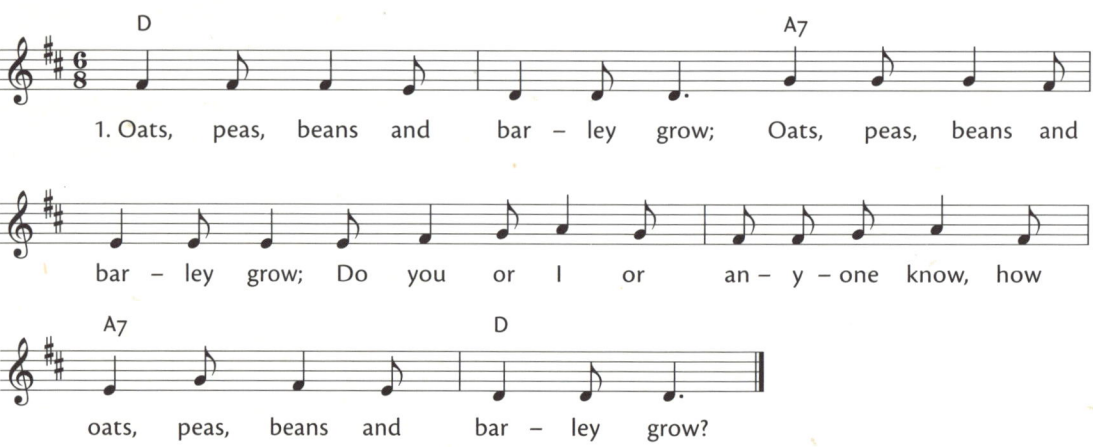

1. Oats, peas, beans and bar-ley grow; Oats, peas, beans and bar-ley grow; Do you or I or an-y-one know, how oats, peas, beans and bar-ley grow?

2. First the farmer sows his seed, Then he stands and takes his ease. (fold arms)
   Stamps his foot and claps his hand, And turns around to view the land. (shade eyes)

3. Waiting for a partner, Waiting for a partner,
   Open the ring and take one in, And then we'll happily dance and sing.

Haying Circle Play

Polish folk song

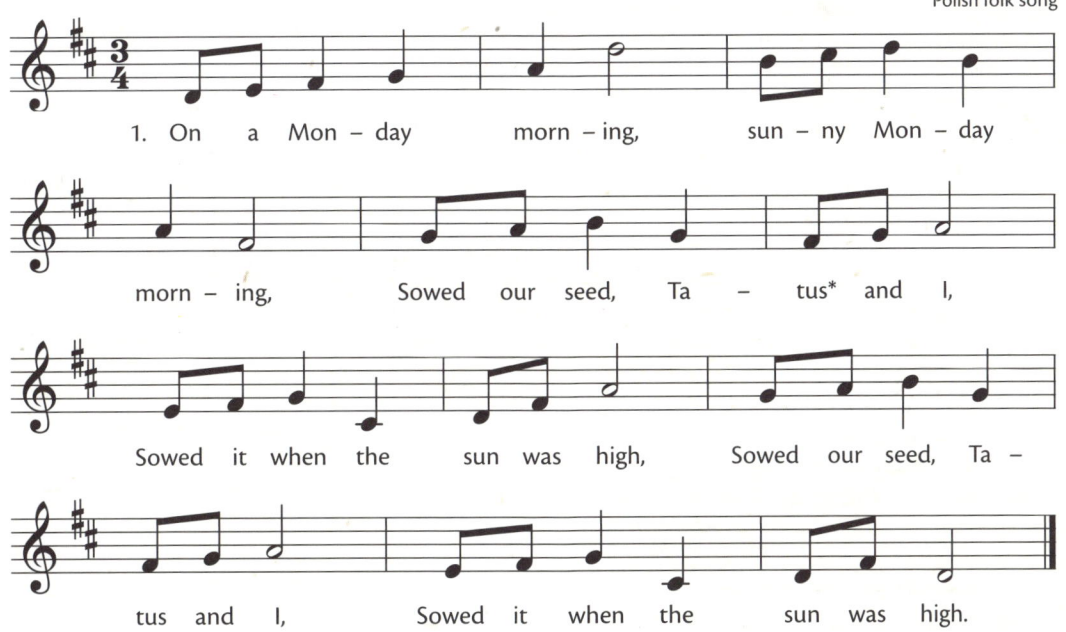

1. On a Monday morning, sunny Monday morning, Sowed our seed, Tatus* and I, Sowed it when the sun was high, Sowed our seed, Tatus and I, Sowed it when the sun was high.

* pronounced Ta-toosh – Polish for 'father'

2. On a Tuesday morning, sunny Tuesday morning,
   Mowed our hay, Tatus and I,
   Mowed it when the sun was high…
   (large, rhythmical cutting of the scythe)

3. On a Wednesday morning…
   Dried our hay, Tatus and I…
   (bend from waist, reach down to gather hay,
   then toss it high)

4. On a Thursday morning…
   Raked our hay, Tatus and I…
   (large, rhythmical raking gesture)

5. On a Friday morning…
   Hauled our hay, Tatus and I…
   (scoop up hay in arms, then drop
   it into 'wagon')

6. On a Saturday morning…
   Sold our hay, Tatus and I…
   (offer hay in outstretched arms)

7. On a Sunday morning…
   Bowed our heads, Tatus and I…
   Thanked the Lord who dwells on high…
   (bow heads, fold hands or cross arms
   in gratitude)

THE LITTLE POT THAT WAS ALWAYS FULL

The following Norse folk tale is a good story to tell at this time of year.

There was once a little house which leaned so badly it was about to fall down. In it lived a young woman. She had spent her last penny and used up all her food. She had one little pot, and it was empty.

The young woman washed the little pot clean and placed it by the door to dry in the sun.

Suddenly, when the young woman wasn't looking the little pot jumped down the steps and ran pell-mell down the street!

It ran to the butcher's shop, and there the butcher's helper, a young man, was cutting up meat for soup. The pot stayed for a while, and then it ran back to the little house and knocked on the door.

The young woman heard the knocking and called, "Who's there?"

"Little Full-Pot."

"Little pot, what's that inside you?"

"Look inside."

"Soup-meat and fat! Who gave it to you?"

"The table was too small and it fell in."

"Oh, you good little pot. Come in and we will cook it."

The young woman took the soup-meat and began to cook it so that it sizzled, and the little house began to dance with joy. The lovely smell rose up the chimney.

The next morning, the young woman once again washed the little pot and put it on the steps to dry. And once again, it jumped down the steps and ran pell-mell down the street.

This time it ran to the baker's shop and there the baker's boy was shaking fresh-baked biscuits out onto the table.

The pot stayed for a while, then ran back and knocked on the door.

"Who's there?"

"Little Full-Pot."

"Little pot, what's that inside you?"

"Look inside!"

"Biscuits! Who gave them to you?"

"The table was too small and they fell in."

"Oh, good little pot, come in and we will eat."

The young woman took the biscuits out of the pot, brewed sweet coffee and drank and ate so happily that the little house again began to dance for joy, and delicious smells poured out of the chimney.

By early the next day she had already washed the little pot and put it out to dry on the steps. This time the little pot ran to the inn, and there the peasants were sitting and paying their coins.

Not long afterward, it came back again and knocked on the door.

"Who's there?"

"Little Full-Pot."

"Little pot, what's that inside you?"

"Look inside!"

"Real gold coins! Who gave them to you?"

"The table was too small and they fell in."

"Oh, good little pot. Come right in and we will count the money."

The young woman took the pot and shook out all the coins and turned them over and over so that the little house again danced for joy, and the last bit of smoke went out the chimney.

The young woman was very happy. But she wanted more.

Why should I wait until tomorrow morning to send the little pot? she thought. *It can bring me something more today.* So without washing the little pot, she just put it out on the steps.

And indeed the little pot began to run. It leaped down the steps and ran down the street until it came to the marketplace. And it stood there. The market had ended and some little mice had collected what was left over.

A little mouse slipped into the little pot to take a nap, and the little pot went home very softly and quietly, and knocked on the door.

"Who's there?"

"Little Full-Pot."

"Oh, good little pot, come in quickly." *What do you have this time,* thought the young woman as she reached curiously into the pot. And out sprang the mouse.

"Oh, you bad little pot!" cried the young woman and she was so angry that she threw the little pot out the door, and it broke into pieces.

The young woman was immediately sorry. "I have nothing! What shall I do now?" she cried.

Fortunately, an older woman was passing by and heard her cry. Taking pity on the young woman, she said, "I need someone to help on my farm. Would you like to work with me?"

And that was what happened, and the young woman became happy again.

OCTOBER

Weaving round objects

To weave a round or oval object — a place mat, pan holder, beehive or house slippers, for example — we need long, slender twigs or shoots that can be built up in layers. These are best worked when fresh. The new shoots of the plum tree, maple, lime and hazelnut serve very well. Sew them together using a blunt needle and heavy craft thread. This work is appropriate for children from the first grade (6–7 years old) on.

Place mats made from wood can be finished with a woven edge. Drill holes in the plywood, pull the plaiting material through them, and then weave around the edge.

Older children can make beautiful toys or practical items such as a miniature baby carriage. For the bottom you will need a piece of thin plywood, to which the poles are attached. Two axles with two wheels each are attached to the bottom, and the sides and tops are woven of some fine material. Finally, insert the handle of the carriage.

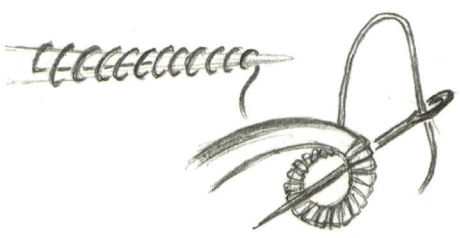

Begin with a switch: start the oval pattern with very young flexible willow switches; with reeds; with very long, new straw; or other hard grasses. Bend one strand of the material into the desired form, then lay another strand on top and attach it with the 'Indian stitch' or the 'simple stitch'.

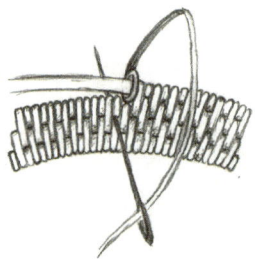

Indian stitch: this stitch requires much patience since the stitches are very close to each other. It results in a very stable piece of work.

Simple stitch: the 'simple stitch' is more difficult but can be used by very dexterous children.

BASKET-MAKING

October is still golden and children can comfortably work in the garden until the end of the month. It's a good time to take stock of the garden, noting which plants are thriving and have even grown out of control. These are ideal for trimming and using for projects like basket-making and shelter-building.

Making baskets with plant materials gives a wonderful feeling of being connected with the natural world. Basketry is one of the oldest types of handicraft. In earlier cultures, human beings used baskets to carry home grains, nuts, berries, herbs, wood and many other items that they harvested or collected.

Take children along on the search for materials, to help them learn about the shape, colour, form and structure of plants. The characteristics of different materials indicate the way they can be used. Be careful not to pick plants that are rare and always ensure that enough is left for the plant to grow luxuriantly again next season.

Climbing and creeping plants

clematis, evergreens, honeysuckle, ivy
October is the best time to harvest these plants. The young creepers are just beginning to turn woody and are still flexible. They already have a certain stability and strength. If the material is breaking easily, soak it in warm water before use.

Tree shoots

maple, willow, ash, hazelnut, apple, plum and other fruit trees
The shoots that have grown over the summer provide strong and attractively coloured material for basketry. Mixing green and red shoots can produce especially beautiful effects.

Grasses and grass-like plants

wheat, rye, oats, barley, corn/maize, sea grass, rushes, reeds, iris, sword lily
Cereal grain stalks should be harvested during the grain harvest, that is, at the end of July. They can be used immediately, but you must allow for substantial drying and shrinkage that will make the basket quite open. Alternatively, you can store and dry the stalks. To make them flexible again, soak them for two hours in lukewarm water.

Grass, lily leaves, corn/maize and rushes need to be worked when newly harvested.

Roots

Tree roots are best collected when a storm has blown down trees. For older children, a visit with adults to such a place can be an unforgettable experience.

Bark

maple, lime, willow, white birch, cherry, hemlock, pine
When a tree has been cut down, ideally in early spring, strip pieces of bark that are as long as possible using a draw-knife. The best bark is from young trees.

Willow hanging basket

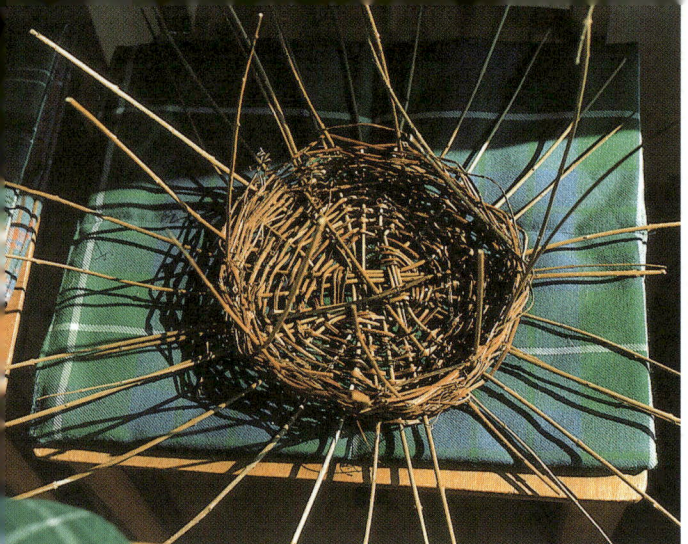

Basket base and the beginning of the side. The spokes of young privet shoots are interwoven with wild grape tendrils.

> **You will need**
> - a sturdy knife
> - a small pair of pliers or tweezers
> - a basketry awl for making space to insert a new shoot

Newly-cut willow shoots must be soaked in water for two or three weeks before use.

Begin the willow basket with a cross base, a star base, or a rectangular base. (See illustrations opposite.) When the bottom is finished, bend the shoots 90 degrees and weave the sides of the basket. To finish off the lip of the basket, cut the shoots, moisten them again, then bend and weave them back into the basket.

With a little help, even four-year-olds can weave a flower basket. In the photo on the left, shoots of a privet hedge are being used as the spokes for a frame and wild grape creepers are woven through them. The bottom is laid out as a star base; it then develops a rounded ball form, and finally comes to a point.

Because the base and the sides are not woven separately, this is an excellent project for children.

Star base

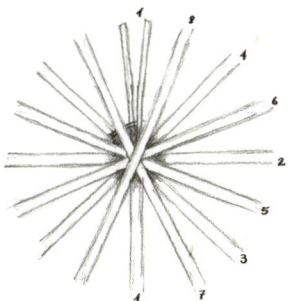

1. Laying the base of spokes

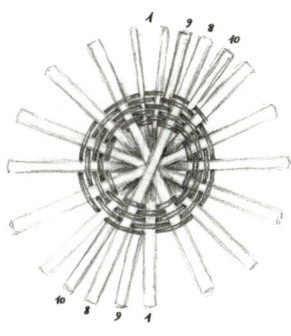

2. Fixing the spokes in place by weaving

Rectangular base

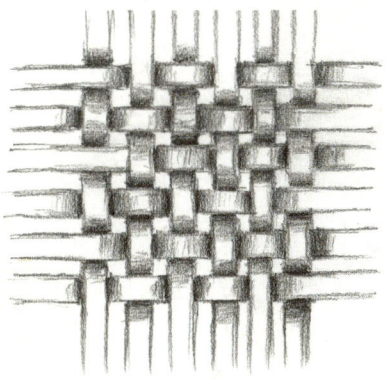

Finishing the lip of the basket

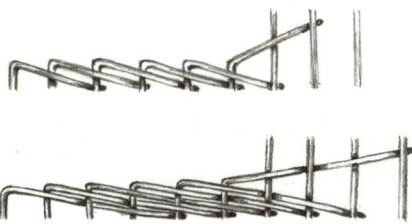

To make the lip of the basket very stable, it is important to soak the material so it doesn't crack when bent.

Japanese-style base (cross base)

  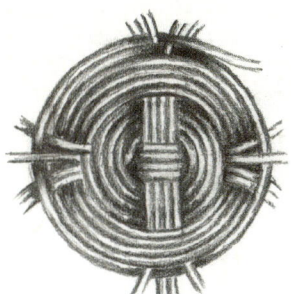

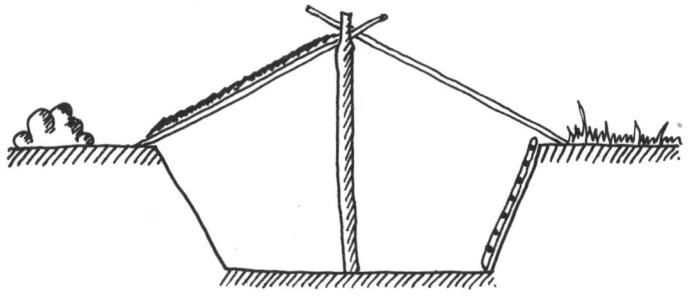

Trench house, with a roof of animal skins over a wood frame. (To build the model, use fir or pine branches for the roof.)

Tent: pole frame covered with animal skins.

Brushwood tent: built with sapling trunks, branches, grasses, moss, reeds and other such materials.

Woven tent: made of strong wooden poles with flexible smaller branches woven in.

Round stonehouse mortared with mud: the roof is made from a stone slab or a piece of wood.

HOUSE-BUILDING

Once the craft of basketry has been mastered, it can be used to make a shelter or little house. Everyone can be involved. It is a basic human need to build a place to live where one can find shelter from the heat and icy cold, from the rain and wind.

When building a shelter, people typically use the materials in their immediate environment. Walls may be made of animal skins or brushwood, woven plant materials, stone or mud. Wood is usually used for the roof, covered with animal skins, straw, grass or bark.

The illustrations here show examples that can be constructed in miniature or built on a large scale outdoors. Projects like these, and the example on the pages that follow, are usually intergenerational, requiring a mix of skill and experience. But you can start by asking children: what makes a home cosy? What is comfortable? What kind of space would you like to create? Working with their hands, children will quickly take ownership of their created space – even if it is very small.

Wattle and daub house: walls of woven wood plastered with mud, roof of logs covered with sod.

House with gabled roof: wicker house with forked poles supporting a pointed roof.

↑ Deep holes must be dug into the earth…

↑ Sturdy bundles of willow branches are tied together.

↓ and wait to be used.

↓ Little bundles of branches are used for stabilisation.

AN INTERGENERATIONAL BUILDING PROJECT

Building an arbour in a partially paved schoolyard.

↑ *Many hands are necessary to carry the willow bundles to the site.*

↓ *The construction is already taking shape.*

↑ *Many hands make the work go fast.*

↓ *The 'roof star' came out especially well.*

Top left: Rapunzel's tower: architectural elements from different cultures (German, Argentinian and Nepalese) overcame language and cultural barriers.

Top right: House of the red sun: in this structure the Japanese influence is very clear.

Left: The Ikebana arbour.

MODEL HOUSES

All the materials used came from the builders' immediate environment.

Below: A Christmas crêche.

Right: A solid but inviting castle made of stones and mud.

Below right: Festival of the flower children: this little girl used beech twigs for a north African mud construction.

NOVEMBER

NORTH WIND

CARING FOR BIRDS

With the end of the growing season, work in the garden comes to a temporary halt. But in the surroundings of every kindergarten — even if it is in a city — will be several varieties of native birds.

As natural habitats are destroyed, birds look for places to feed, breed and nest in human residential areas.

Such areas can include bushes that produce berries such as rosehip, sloe and elderberry. Here birds can find insects, seeds from trees and grasses, worms and many other kinds of food.

Trees and hedges provide nesting places, but it's important to differentiate between birds that nest in holes, and those that nest in the open. Finches make their nests in the open, in trees, bushes and hedges. The blackbird, with its beautiful song, does as well.

Most varieties of titmouse — who are especially useful since they eat harmful insects — nest in holes. For them we must provide nesting places by hanging up nesting boxes in trees. Also, don't forget the starlings and the nuthatches: they need nesting boxes with larger holes. Wherever possible, orient the boxes so that the opening looks toward the rising sun.

In autumn, nesting boxes must be cleaned out to get rid of old nesting material and vermin. Sweep out all corners and cracks with a brush. This way, we can give the birds a clean, safe shelter for the cold winter. For more information on nesting boxes, see *Spring and Summer Nature Activities for Waldorf Kindergartens*.

FEEDING BIRDS

The arrival of winter means we need to think about how to help our local birds survive until spring.

Most kindergartens can set up a bird table or feeder near a window. Children can spread grass seeds they have gathered in the summer on it, or plantain, or a commercial birdseed mix. All birds love oat flakes. Even an apple that has begun to go bad can be put out.

It is helpful to keep a patch of grass in the yard free of snow, and also to put out water for the birds. For this, you'll need a flat, frost-proof plate that you fill once or several times a day with warm water during periods of sub-freezing temperature, and the drinking dish must be kept clean.

In the cold of winter birds need fat. You can buy balls of fat or suet wrapped in a wire mesh that can be hung in a tree. Birds also like scrap fat from the butcher's shop: put a handful-sized piece in a nylon mesh bag (the kind oranges are often sold in) and hang it in a tree.

Top left: During the winter it is important to keep areas of grass free of snow so that the birds who feed on the ground can find something to eat.

Clockwise from top right: This is a good method of making bird food using seeds that the birds would find in their environment. In a clay flower pot complete with perches, the feed stays clean.

Making your own bird food

Natural winter food for birds should be gathered in late summer and autumn, and thoroughly dried.

Along paths you'll find stalks of grains and seed-bearing grasses, including stinging nettle, yarrow, St John's wort and white ox-eye.

From the edge of the forest, gather seeds from the black and red elderberry, sloe, rosehip and hawthorn, and seed cones from pine, larch, spruce and fir.

To make birdfeed, make a fire in an appropriate fireplace. Then take 6–10 pounds (3–5 kg) of vegetable margarine or coconut fat, melt it in a large pot, and mix in the dried seeds that you have gathered until all are covered with fat. Let the mixture cook briefly at a high temperature. This prevents mould from forming later on.

Next, get your clay flower pots ready. While the mixture is cooling in the cooking pot, attach branches to flower pots to serve as perches for the birds. Tie the branches with string and make a loop for hanging the feeder on a tree.

Finally, fill the flower pots with the mixture, compact it well, and let the pot stand until the bird food mixture has hardened. Start feeding the birds as soon as the snow arrives.

Modelling with beeswax

At this cold time of year it is a real blessing for children to be able to do modelling with warm, aromatic beeswax. Give them enough wax so that they can work with both hands and have enough to make a little house.

For a kindergarten group of 25 children, you need at least 9 pounds (4 kg) of beeswax.

Put 2 pounds (1 kg) of pure beeswax in an enamelled pan (preferably a flat one), place in an oven heated to 150 °F/70 °C, and let it melt. Stir in 2 ounces (60 g) of lanolin (*adeps lanae*, available from a pharmacy). Let the mixture slowly cool until it is hard. Remove the hardened wax with a wooden spoon and place on wax/greaseproof paper. Then break the wax into 'dumplings' that are the right size for the hands of the children. Put these back into the flat pot. Wax prepared in this way can be remelted many times.

An hour to an hour and a half before the modelling session, warm the wax in the oven at 125 °F/50 °C — being careful that it doesn't melt.

A wooden board or a cross-section of a tree trunk make good work surfaces.

Beeswax mixed with lanolin stays malleable for 15 to 30 minutes, then becomes hard and stable. Many little works of art can be made from beeswax. This wonderfully aromatic, precious material appeals to the children's impulse to give something form and to experience the joy of creation.

BEESWAX

Beeswax is a precious material. It's good for children to understand how the bees have laboured long and hard all summer to make wax and honey.

When honeycombs are removed from the hive, they are placed in a honey centrifuge and spun to extract the honey. The honey flows like liquid gold to the bottom of the centrifuge and through several fine sieves. A rich, delicious odour fills the room. What remains is the precious wax; the wax combs are gathered and put in the melter. Impurities are caught in the sieve as the wax runs down into the collecting tray.

Left: A solar wax melter with many pieces of honeycomb.
Below: Looking into the honey centrifuge.

The wax is melted in an enamelled metal container, in a water bath.

Instead of a table, a long bench can be used for dipping. This helps maintain a fixed order as the children walk slowly around the bench. As they walk, they can sing songs about autumn, winter and Advent.

Tips for dipping candles

- Don't overfill the dipping pot with cold wax because the wax expands when it is melted. It is better to add more later.
- Melt slowly, first over a very low heat that is slowly increased. It is very important that the pot for the hot water is almost as tall as the container holding the wax.
- Put the container in the water pot and fill the pot until the water almost comes up to the lip of the container. It takes about an hour and a half for wax to melt in a water bath.
- The wax at the bottom of the container will melt and want to expand, while the top layer is still hard, hindering the boiling. Therefore, under no circumstances should the top layer be pressed down. There is a danger that the hot bottom wax will shoot up like a geyser!
- For uniform melting, place two or three pieces of bent wire into the wax-container. Something made from a metal that conducts heat, such as a piece of steel pipe, will also serve. This will allow the already-melted wax at the bottom to rise to the top. The metal objects can be removed when all the wax has begun to melt.
- Never try to melt the wax in a pot directly on the burner without the water bath. This creates a serious fire hazard.
- In candle-dipping, it is extremely important to maintain discipline and order among the children to prevent them from being injured by the hot, molten wax.

DIPPING CANDLES

Making candles out of pure beeswax is a peaceful activity in the Advent season. Candle-making is also an opportunity to involve children in the careful creation of gifts with real value.

For one candle about 5 inches (12 cm) long and half an inch (1.5 cm) in diameter (the size of a Christmas tree candle), you will need about ⅔ of an ounce (20 g) of beeswax and about 7 inches (18 cm) of sturdy wick cord.

For the dipping process, you need twice as much wax as will go into the candles, so if you want to make 25 to 30 candles, you will need 3 to 4 pounds (1.5–2 kg) of beeswax.

Children can manage candle-dipping best after they have been out playing in the fresh cold air. They'll be happy to be inside in the warm room and will be able to control their limbs. The candle-dipping can then be a harmonising experience.

If children don't have enough patience to finish their candles during one dipping session, the work can be spread out over several days. This has the advantage that the unfinished candles can harden and cool and will 'grow' more quickly and easily when they are dipped again (this is because the melted wax adheres better to an underlayer of cold, hardened wax).

Once the wax has melted, place the pot with the water bath, with the wax-container in it, on a hot plate in the middle of the circle or on a table. One by one the children can dip their candle in the melted wax, holding it by a loop in the wick at the top, and then letting the wax drip off and cool.

After five to seven dippings, the growing candle should be allowed to harden thoroughly. The best thing is to hang them on a stand made from the top of a small tree or to string them on a wooden pole and to take them outside for a time. Keep the wax warm on the stove.

After about fifteen dippings, the candles should have become thick enough to use. If so, they can be shortened by cutting off about half an inch from the bottom.

Candle-dipping outside, in the dark and cold, over a campfire, can be a very special experience.

The children carefully and lovingly wrap the candles they have made. They have created these Christmas gifts with patience and joy.

You will need

- a varied collection of paper: flyers, egg cartons, packing paper, etc.
- a three-gallon (10 litre) bucket
- a pulp vat: a wash tub or similar
- for each child: a cloth made of cotton, felt or fleece that is slightly larger than the pulp frames
- a sponge
- pulp frames consisting of a flat sieve in a frame. A large round wire sieve used in the kitchen to extract oil from spray can be used, as can sturdy window screening cut to size
- a kitchen blender
- textile remnants (rags and thread from natural textiles such as linen, cotton, wool or hemp)
- dried plants and dried plant fibres
- stirring stick or kitchen spoon
- a drying rack or clothesline
- boards for pressing
- a lot of absorbent newspaper
- two fairly large clamps
- cleaning rags, scrubbing brushes and a bucket for the floor

Collect used paper

You'll be amazed with the variety you find: packaging, writing paper, drawing paper, painting paper, book paper, newspapers, brochures and so on.

Sort it

Take out the things that can be reused, such as paper bags, cardboard boxes and re-usable envelopes.

Then take out all paper that is covered with black print. Too much printer's ink makes it impossible to give the paper a clear colour.

Remove synthetics

Remove all paper that has glue or a self-sealing band on it, staples or fasteners.

Tear it up

Reduce all the paper to coin-sized pieces.

This rather noisy work tells us a lot — through the senses of touch, hearing and sight — about the structure of different kinds of paper. The children

MAKING PAPER

With the end of the growing season in November and the coming of the winter, paper-making is another excellent activity for children. Plants are dying; most of the organic substances in the plants have disintegrated and what remains is primarily the cellulose that gives the plant its structure. Cellulose fibers from grasses, ferns, stinging nettles and the leaves of local trees can be used in paper-making.

Making paper is a watery business! For that reason, you will need a room with a waterproof floor and furniture that is not easily damaged. A spacious kindergarten washroom, a recreation hall, the school kitchen or a clear area in the garden would serve well. If you work outside at this time of year, fill the pulp vat with warm water to make the work more pleasant and ensure that the children don't get cold hands.

can play guessing games, closing their eyes and trying to decide what type of paper is being ripped up. The children spur each other on, especially when many sit in a circle around a mountain of paper and there are many containers nearby for the little pieces of paper.

Tip If you need a large quantity of old paper for a festival or large gathering when many children will be making paper, ask at your local city hall. There is usually a large amount of paper available that has been put through a paper shredder. Such paper is very good for paper-making.

Soak and blend it

Pour water over the paper that has been torn into small pieces and let it soak for one day.

Then break it down by putting it, in small portions, in a kitchen blender. The finer the paper mix, the more homogenous the end product will be. If you want to maintain certain patterns or colours from the used paper, don't break it up too much.

Soak different types of paper in separate containers to reduce them in size to varying degrees. For example, egg cartons and corrugated cardboard can be very finely 'puréed', while used gift wrap can be left larger so the colour is retained.

Plant ingredients

Soak dried grasses, leaves or pressed flowers for about half an hour and put them in the pulp vat at the end.

The dipping frames are held horizontally when they are taken out of the pulp vat and are shaken gently back and forth so that the water runs off.

The dipped sheet of paper is carefully turned upside down onto the fleece cloth. Excess water is removed with a sponge.

The dipping frame is carefully removed and the sheet of dipped paper remains on the cotton under-cloth.

Finally the cloth with the dipped paper is hung on the drying stand.

Textile ingredients

Material from cotton, wool and linen remnants should be put in at the very end.

Prepare the pulp mixture

Prepare the pulp mixture in a large, low container. As a general guideline, put in about 10 quarts (10 litres) of water to 1 quart (1 litre) of pulp mixture. Other proportions will also work and you'll need to experiment to find what works best for you with each particular batch of paper. Now add any plant and textile ingredients.

Dip the paper

On top of a pile of newspaper next to the pulp vat, put the cotton or felt cloth and smooth it out. Place the dipping frame so that the sieve is on top and is covered by the frame.

Before you dip the frame, stir the paper mixture vigorously with a ladle or a kitchen spoon.

Put the frame vertically into the vat at the far side and draw it towards the body; then turn it to the horizontal and carefully lift it out of the water. Gently shake the frame back and forth to distribute the paper evenly on the sieve and let the water run off.

After the water has run off, carefully lift the frame. Put one corner of the sieve frame on the lower edge of the cloth and tip the frame over very carefully, depositing the paper onto the cloth. Press gently on the frame so that much of the water is absorbed by the underlying layer of newspapers. Careful sponging can speed up this process.

Dry the paper

Put another cloth and several sheets of newspaper on the newly dipped sheet and the fleece underlayer, and compress the whole pile with a rolling pin.

Now hang the cloth with the newly dipped sheet out to dry on the line. When the sheet is fully dry — usually after about two days — separate it from the cloth and iron it between two sheets of newspaper.

> **Tip** Several sheets can be dried at once by stacking them with their fleece cloths and newspaper sheets between two flat pieces of wood, holding them together with clamps. The newspaper soaks up a lot of water so the drying process is greatly accelerated.

Natural adhesives

Paste and plaster can join together many natural materials. Light-weight objects such as leaves, grass, moss and feathers can be held together or attached to a sheet of paper with paste. Paste will also hold grains of sand on a piece of paper to create a beautiful landscape. If you add natural colouring to the paste, it can be used for finger painting. Heavy materials, such as stones, seashells, twigs and fruit, hold together with a homemade dough or plaster material such as beeswax.

Make your own paste

To make your own paste, use a granular powder called methyl cellulose. It works well in craft projects and is totally non-toxic. It can be purchased in building supply stores. Put a teaspoon of the powder in a glass jar and mix it with 2 ounces (50 ml) of cold water. In thirty minutes, the paste is ready to be used. It will keep in the refrigerator for one to two weeks.

Finger-painting

First make the paste as described on the left, then mix with coloured water. The coloured water can be made from a powder or by decoction. For the powder, cut up the various plant materials — leaves, stems, bark and fruits — and mash them with a mortar and pestle. Decoction is similar to making tea: put the pieces of plant that are to provide the colour into hot water. The water becomes coloured and the plant material can be strained out. Take two tablespoons of this coloured liquid, add 2 ounces (50 ml) of water, and pour this into a jar. Mix the water and colour well and then add one teaspoon of paste. The intensity of the plant colour depends on the strength of the decoction and how much it has been diluted. In half an hour, the paste will have thickened enough to be used for finger painting. It will keep in the refrigerator for one to two weeks.

Colours

green

stinging nettles or spinach leaves
Mash 4 ounces (100 g) of fresh nettles or spinach leaves and boil in 2 ounces (50 ml) of water. Allow to steep for one hour and then remove the leaves.

red

beetroot juice
Cook red beetroots and keep the water.

blue

blueberry juice
Pass the fresh blueberries through a sieve.

PAINTING AND HANDICRAFTS

The activities in this section go well with paper-making and are ideal indoor activities in colder months. Natural materials are best, and children are very creative with even simple objects like twigs, fruit, seashells, stones and bark.

Avoid using conventional adhesives that contain solvents and preservatives. Make your own, or find other ways to hold things together, such as yarn, wire, grass, dough or nails.

brown

black tea or the brown outer leaves of an onion
Take the brown leaves from four or five onions, mix with 2 ounces (50 ml) of water and bring to the boil. Allow to steep until the water turns brown.

violet

elderberry juice

yellow

powdered saffron or decoction of sorrel
Make a decoction of the coloured mignonette using about 4 ounces (100 g). A half-teaspoon of saffron powder mixed with 2 ounces (50 ml) of water will also work well.

An advantage of homemade finger paints is that you not only create the colour and determine its intensity, but you can also vary the thickness of the paint. If the paint is too thin, pour in a bit more paste and wait until it has thickened. If it is too thick, thin it with water or some of the coloured liquid.

A disadvantage is that the colours are not very intense. Use bright white heavy paper or a white bed sheet as a background rather than a piece of window glass. Also, dilute the coloured decoction or the powder as little as possible.

Sand pictures

First sift the sand — obtained from the beach, a building supply centre or elsewhere — through a large kitchen sieve to remove stones and plant material. Catch the sand in a bucket and then put it into jars. Now the colouring can begin. Use the same coloured fluids used to make finger paints.

The sand must be thoroughly soaked with the coloured water, juice or dye. Mix the coloured fluid with the sand in the jars using a spoon, then spread it on newspaper and let it dry outside. It can be put back into jars and, if thoroughly dried and stored in a dark place, it will keep for several years. Naturally-coloured sandy soil can be sieved and stored in jars. This can add natural brown tones to the picture.

You can also collect assorted nuts (acorns, birch seeds and so on), seashells, twigs, leaves and moss. After being dried, all of these will keep well and can be used in their dried state.

A landscape can be 'painted' using sands of different colours and the collected natural materials. Apply a brushful of paste onto a large sheet of paper and sprinkle on the sand. If the paper is picked up and gently shaken, the loose grains of sand will roll onto the paste. Each colour should be applied with a separate application of paste onto the paper.

Then paste the other materials that have been collected onto the paper. Special effects can be created with larger stones, seashells and plant fibres.

Pan pipes

Pan pipes can be made out of a piece of bamboo about 2 feet (60 cm) long. The inner diameter of the bamboo tube should be about ½ inch (1 cm). Scrape out any soft matter and saw the bamboo into five to eight pieces. The first piece should be at least 4 inches (10 cm) long. Each additional piece should be ½ inch (1 cm) longer than the previous one.

Although a length of bamboo is hollow, it does have thickened joints where the tube is blocked. When the bamboo is sawn into pieces, the joints should be retained so that each tube of the pan pipe has an open end and a closed end.

Tie the pipes together tightly, in order of length, with a piece of strong cord just below the open end. Then tie together the other ends with another length of cord.

Castanets

To make castanets you need two wooden spoons. Saw off the handles of the spoons but leave about ¾ inch (1.5 cm) just above the bowl of the spoon. Smooth away the saw marks with sandpaper and drill a hole in the handle of each spoon. Tie the two pieces together with a piece of coloured yarn or string so that the two hollow sides of the spoon face each other. The castanets can be coloured with finger paints.

Nature mobile

Attach natural objects to a tree branch.

- ✪ In spring, bright ribbons, a hazelnut twig in flower, feathers and little animals cut from wood can be hung on the branch.
- ✪ In summer, use seashells, dried flowers and holiday mementos.
- ✪ In autumn, use nuts, leaves of different colours and feathers.
- ✪ In winter, you might decorate the branch with ivy, evergreens, straw stars, bright ribbons and assorted nuts.

DECEMBER

An enchanted world: the round benches of a willow hut covered in white.

The seed-bearing plants in a herb spiral are a winter food source for birds.

Advent wreath

Children love making an Advent wreath, and the whole room fills with the fragrance of the pine branches.

Use branches from trees that don't drop their needles as much (for example, Douglas fir, Nordman fir or the common pine). You can also add other evergreens, such as boxwood, cherry laurel and ivy, into the wreath.

Cut off lengths of about 8 inches (20 cm). Overlap the larger branches, binding them with wire as you go to form a stable ring as the base of the wreath. Then place the finer branches onto the base in layers, and secure with wire.

This pre-Christmas period is filled with secrets, surprises and little gifts. Children love discovering that the wreath has been decorated for the first Advent Sunday, if possible with four handsome beeswax candles.

This poem can accompany the lighting of the Advent wreath:

The gift of light I thankfully hold
And pass to my neighbour, its shining gold
That everyone may feel its glow,
Receiving and giving, may love and grow.

ADVENT

Winter is a good time for getting a different perspective on everyday outdoor objects. See how different the garden looks with snow piled on the fence posts, with the last berries on the bushes wearing little snow caps, and with benches or the sandbox buried and white. It's also interesting to notice how many variations of whiteness there are in the snow: it can be a cold red in the morning, blinding in the glistening midday sun, and have a blue shimmer at dusk. Our own shadows, or those of trees, can seem to stretch on endlessly in the low sunlight.

Now is the time of Advent, a period of contemplation and expectation. The darkness becomes deeper, and the outer world colder. People begin to prepare for Christmas, Diwali, Hanukkah and other winter festivals.

AN ADVENT STORY

Far away in the East there lived a very good man called Bishop Nicholas. One day, he was told that there was a city in the West where everyone was starving, even the children. He called together all his servants and said, "Bring me the food from your gardens and your fields so that we can stop the children from starving."

The servants brought apples and nuts in baskets, and on top they placed honey cakes. Others brought wheat grain in sacks. Bishop Nicholas had all the food loaded onto a ship with white and blue sails, as white as the clouds and as blue as Bishop Nicholas's coat.

The wind blew the sails and the ship moved quickly over the water. When the wind was tired, the sailors pulled at the oars and rowed the ship to the city in the West. They travelled for seven days and seven nights.

When they arrived in the city, it was evening. There was no one in the streets, but lights burned in the windows of the houses. Bishop Nicholas knocked at a window. The mother in the house thought it was a late wanderer, and her child opened the door. But there was no one there. The child ran to the window, but there was no one there either.

But a basket was there, filled with apples and nuts and honey cake. Next to the basket was a sack with golden wheat grains spilling out. Baskets with apples, nuts and honey cake and sacks with wheat grains stood in front of the doors of the other houses too. The people in the city ate the presents and became healthy and happy again.

St Nicholas died a long time ago. But every year on his birthday he makes a trip back to earth. He orders his white horse and rides from star to star, bringing gifts to children. Where Nicholas cannot go himself, he lends his voice to good people and asks them to deliver, in his name, apples, nuts and honey cake.

Blooming branches

Around the start of December (in Germany, this is done on St Barbara's Day on December 4), cut branches from a cherry, apple, plum or almond tree, or from a forsythia bush, winter jasmine or horse chestnut. Place them overnight in lukewarm water then put them in a jug of water in a moderately warm room. Change the water every three days, and trim the branches from time to time. The branches will bloom on Christmas Day, making a wonderful display for the children to remember.

Rattling walnuts

For each child, split a walnut into two perfect halves, hollow it out, paint it gold and fill it with wheat grains, which have been saved as seeds for the coming spring. Place a loop of thread between the walnut halves and glue them back together. When the children shake the nuts, they'll hear a mysterious rattling. In German-speaking cultures, this is part of the celebration of St Nicholas Day on December 6: St Nicholas tells the children that it's a secret why the nut rattles, and that the secret will last until Easter when they can open the nuts. Children can take the nuts home and hang them on the Christmas tree.

It's important for a teacher or parent to present the rattling walnuts as a mysterious thing; a scientific explanation would only dispel the magic. If you think that the magic might not survive the trip home, the nuts can be used to decorate a branch in the classroom, until spring arrives.

Blowing ships

Walnuts can also be used to make small boats which can be blown across a container filled with water and other obstacles to create shipping lanes.

If you're able to plan a year's worth of activities leading up to the making of a Christmas scene, you might find this schedule useful:

✪ In January, create human and animal figures out of wool. They appear in the Christmas scene as Mary with the child, Joseph, the shepherds and the kings.
✪ In February, build the stable from round sticks. Candleholders and vases can also be made from clay.
✪ In March, sow the grain from the rattling walnuts. Use straw to make stars for the dark pine branches.
✪ In April, designate the area in the garden where the poinsettia will grow.
✪ In May, use natural plant dyes to dye the cloth for the base and backdrop.
✪ In June, fill a pot-pourri bag with rose petals and save the nicest butterfly cocoons.
✪ In July, when you're on country walks, collect beautiful objects from the mineral, plant and animal worlds.
✪ In August, harvest the straw for the cradle.
✪ In September, choose a few fragrant winter apples from the tree.
✪ In October, weave a small cradle basket or build a simple hut from natural materials to serve as the stable.
✪ In November, make beeswax candles to light the Christmas scene.
✪ In December, bring everything together. An entire yearly cycle, in which the children have been actively involved, comes to an end before their very eyes.

CHRISTMAS SCENES

A Christmas scene is a wonderful way to present an overview of annual themes in nature, and is therefore ideal for helping children to understand the end of the calendar year.

Every morning during Advent, children can collect objects to be added to the scene: mineral, plant and animal, and coloured beeswax can also be used to make Christmas figures. Building a Christmas scene is a communal project: people must listen to each other, and in doing so, they experience the real meaning of the Christmas season.

Above: Roots can be collected to form the structure of a Christmas scene. Children can remove bits of earth and loose material to reveal the intricate detail of the roots; this is best done using a wire brush or an old toothbrush.

Right: Some children like working with wire brushes; others prefer a mallet, chisel, knife or saw (with adult supervision).

JANUARY

Children normally participate in wool workshops with great enthusiasm. The process of obtaining and then working with wool, from the sheep to a ball of wool which can become a woven rug or knitted sweater, is long and full of hard work.

Shearing sheep

Outdoor festivals and agricultural fairs are good places for children to experience sheep shearing. It is a very skillful task involving strength and great care, and is usually done in the summer.

Cleaning and drying the wool

The wool must next be cleaned of all loose dirt. To do this, soak the wool for several hours in a barrel filled with rain water. It must be stirred and beaten a few times, either with old beaters or with bare feet. Hang it up to dry, then carefully pull it apart to release the bits of dirt. Repeat the whole procedure until the wool is nice and clean. Ideally, this task should be done outdoors; the best time is in the summer after the sheep have been sheared.

Washing wool with old beaters.

Tin tubs are good for washing wool outdoors; wash the wool in rainwater or well-water if possible, but remember not to use detergent so as not to remove the lanolin.

WORKING WITH WOOL

January is often cold and wet, so it is a good time to introduce children to working with wool in a warm environment. Clothing made from wool can, due to the open nature and elasticity of the fibres, trap large amounts of air and thereby insulate the body. Wool can also absorb up to forty per cent of its own weight in moisture, without feeling damp, which means sweat doesn't build up on the skin.

Germs and bacteria don't settle on wool, because of the scales on the individual wool hairs. The lanolin in wool also has a healing effect: lanolin is an important base for ointments. Sheared wool is therefore perfect for maintaining a comfortable body temperature. It protects us equally well from cold, moisture and heat.

Carding

The first step in processing the cleaned wool is carding, which loosens up the wool. It can be done without any equipment: simply pull the wool apart with your fingers to make a fine veil. It can be described to children as making the wool thin enough so that light can shine through, or as delicate as a butterfly's wings, or as fine as a snowflake.

Older children can try using hand carders, between which the wool is brushed. The most dexterous children might like to try a carding drum. You need to be careful not to put too much wool between the large and small brushing cylinders. This technique needs a lot of patience to produce a nice thick wool fleece.

Wool can be dried on anything from laundry racks and compost sieves to ladders covered with fishing nets.

Spinning

The next step is to spin the wool. A stick spindle is an easy way to make the carefully carded wool into thread.

To make a stick spindle, take a stick that is 6–8 inches (15–20 cm) long and about ½ inch (1 cm) thick, cut off the bark and sand it smooth.

To spin using a stick spindle, two children must sit opposite each other. One child holds a handful of carded wool, while the other carefully pulls out wool fibres, twists them into a thread in a clockwise direction, and wraps the thread around the stick spindle. Pulling, turning and wrapping should be done rhymically.

Another simple way of spinning is with a branch hook spindle. The branch hook is turned on its long axis with one hand, while the other hand holds the carded wool. This is a good way of spinning very fine, very strong yarn. Even six-year-olds can spin using a branch hook if they've developed enough feeling for the wool beforehand.

Working with a drop spindle is too difficult for children, but it is still worth demonstrating this age-old tool used in many cultures. While the adult forms the thread, the children have great fun keeping the spindle rotating fast enough. As soon as the thread has the right twist, it is wound around the rotating disc or block.

Spinning wool with a branch hook spindle (top).

Spinning thread with a partner is a very good way of learning cooperation (middle).

Spinning with a drop spindle (bottom).

Rhythm and singing

It can be easier for children to learn rhymical skills such as spinning if appropriate songs or rhymes accompany the activity. One five-year-old sensed the connection between singing and working: he refused to start spinning until the right song was sung. He was convinced that the spinning wheel would only start to turn once the children were singing.

Below is a traditional American song that imitates the sound of a quickly spinning wheel.

SARASPONDA

Twisting

When two bobbins are full, the two threads can be twisted together to make a stronger thread. To do this, a new bobbin – onto which the double thread is to be wound – is turned in a counterclockwise direction.

If spun yarn is used as a single ply, or untwisted, thread, the cloth made from it can be easily pulled out of shape, especially after being washed several times.

Threads can be twisted using a stone weight. Take some well-spun thread off a bobbin and divide it in half. Holding the ends of the thread in one hand, place a stone, scissors or other heavy object at the mid-point of the thread. When you release the heavy object, the two threads in your hand will turn very fast and twist themselves into a very strong two-ply string. Children often have a lot of ideas for things to make with this double thread.

Twisting threads with a stone weight.

Before washing, bind the skein together loosely in four places.

Winding a skein

Winding a skein – a loosely-coiled bundle of yarn – is the simplest and best method to keep the twisted wool yarn ready for use.

Wind the yarn around your hand and elbow, and mark the end of the yarn with thread of another colour so that the end can be found easily again later. Children who already understand something about numbers often enjoy counting the number of 'elbows' it takes to wind the thread. Finally, bind the skein together loosely in four places.

Washing the yarn

When washing the yarn, handle it very carefully, as if you were handling a living creature. If children are told that it should be 'bathed like a baby', they are normally especially careful. The yarn also doesn't like sudden changes in temperature, so ensure the water is just slightly warmer than lukewarm.

Place the yarn in water and gently move it back and forth, then hang it up to drip dry. Don't use any detergent because this reduces the natural oil content of the wool.

The drying process can be speeded up by rolling the yarn in towels, pressing it gently and then hanging the yarn to dry loosely in fresh air. It should never be dried in bright sunlight, when the temperature is below freezing, or in other extreme conditions. Turn it frequently so that moisture is able to escape from all over the skein.

Storage

After drying the wool, store it in an airy place, hanging it in skeins if possible. It should be well cared for, turned often, and kept with herb bags to keep the moths away and to give the wool a nice fragrance. Lavender and cedar oil are good protection against moths. Remember that before the wool can be made into something, it must be wound into a ball.

If children wash the wool as gently as if they are washing a baby, the wool will stay soft and loose.

If the yarn is to be used soon, it can be rolled into a ball right away.

Finger crochet

For children, finger crochet is the simplest method of creating something from relatively rough and irregular hand-spun wool yarn. They can crochet for a long time and make extremely strong chains, using them as 'horse reins', or bands to tie objects together, or to put a border around their play areas.

A, B, C, D = *instructions for the basic loop*

D – Pull tight

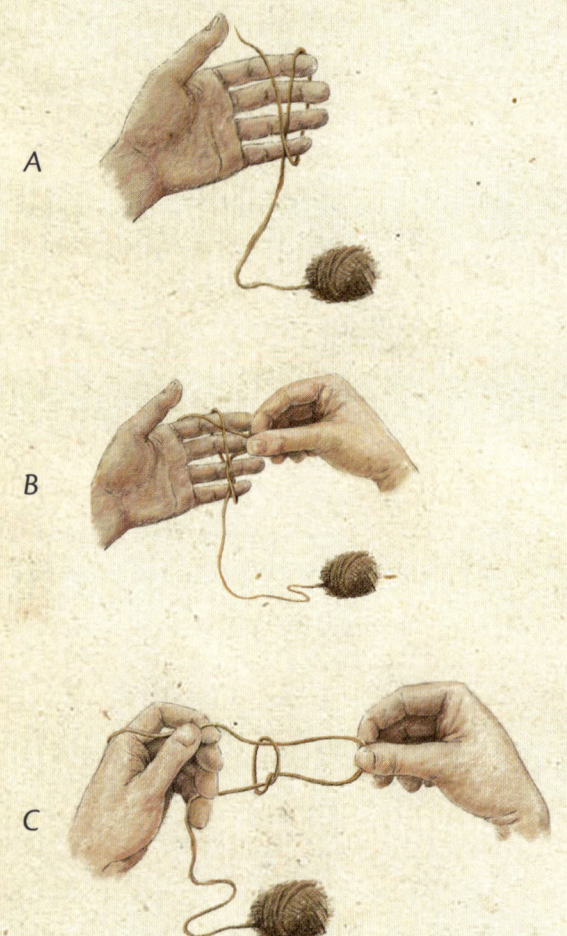

E

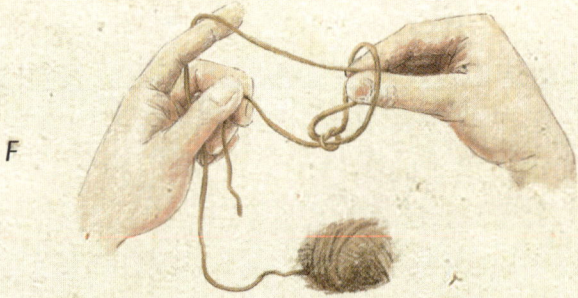

F

E and F can be repeated as many times as you like.

The thread pattern:

A, B, C, D {

E, F {

WEAVING

Weaving is a particularly good activity for children because there are so many options at different skill levels. It can help to keep weaving activities of different skill levels in different physical spaces, to avoid confusion.

Stick table loom

The stick table loom consists of a 20 inch (50 cm) base board, which is fastened to the table edge by two clamps. Wooden dowels are placed in 26 holes, each with a 3/8 inch (10 mm) diameter. Each dowel is 5 1/2 inches (135 mm) long and has a diameter of 3/8 inch (10 mm). The depth of the holes should be 5/8 inch (15 mm). Drill a 1/8 inch (3 mm) hole horizontally, about 6/8 inch (18 mm) from the end of the dowel for the warp thread, which is pulled through the holes.

Place the dowels into the holes of the base board and knot two warp thread pairs (four ends) together. At this point, the children can begin to weave: it is very easy for them to wind the yarn rhythmically back and forth.

When the full length of the dowels has been filled with weaving, remove the dowels from the base board and carefully press down on the woven rows; then replace the dowels onto the base board so that weaving can resume.

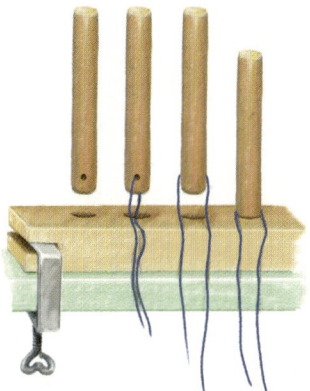

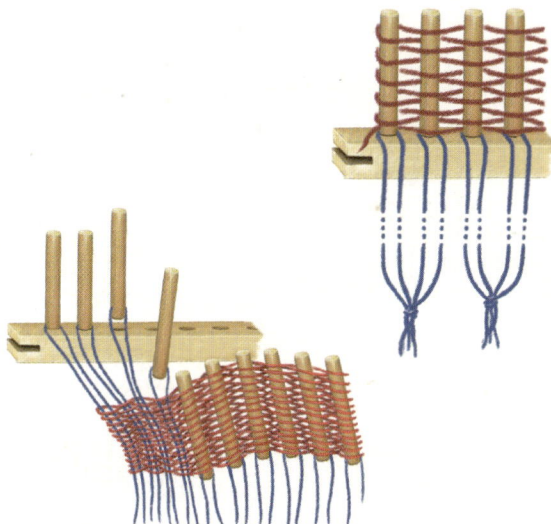

The advantage of this weaving method is that children can create any length of cloth from which rugs, cushion covers, etc. can be made.

Thick, hand-spun, twisted yarn is especially good for this kind of project.

Cardboard loom frame

Cardboard loom frames deserve a special mention because they can be individually made to match the skill of an individual child. Furthermore, the card used can be recycled from old calendars, etc.

Make cuts in the ends of the cardboard about ³/₄ inch (2 cm) long; you can vary the number of cuts and the space between between them. Pull the warp thread tight enough so that the cardboard is slightly curved, which gives the child a handy hollow space for weaving.

Rounded wood loom frame

Children often enjoy sawing, carving, sanding and then nailing together loom frames of notched wood.

Use rounded dry (not green) wood sticks, about ³/₄ inch (2 cm) in diameter and any length.

Cut two long and two short pieces. Carve notches into the ends, and sand all the pieces. Fit the indentations together and secure them with nails. Reinforce all four corners with very strong cord.

For the warp thread, either make small notches or drill fine holes in the two short pieces of the frame. The warp thread can then be pulled through the holes.

Clockwise from top right:

Very long pieces of cloth can be made on stick looms. Many hands push the finished strips toward the near end, doing so in pairs and at the same time from both sides. This way, the rug will be thick, strong and warm.

Cardboard loom frames are easy to make and weaving progress is fast.

Fast progress means the children stay interested for longer.

Thread spun on a stick spindle is ideal for weaving on a stick loom.

The corner joints are held together by nails and cord and warp thread is pulled through small drilled holes.

Card weaving

This technique can be used to weave belts, hair bands, key rings or bookmarks.

To make the weaving card, copy the pattern opposite onto strong cardboard and cut it out. Pull the warp thread through the card; the thread should be the right length for the piece of cloth you want to weave, plus 4–6 inches (10–15 cm) at each end.

Knot the ends of the warp threads together and attach one end to a hook, doorknob or similar object. Using string, attach the other end to the child's body.

Pull the moving set of warp threads to the top of the weaving card, and push the shuttle, also made of cardboard, through the space between the two sets of threads. Next, press the threads to the bottom of the card, and push the shuttle back through in the opposite direction. Repeat until your cloth is the desired length.

The warp threads are connected to the body at the right-hand end, and it's the body which maintains the tension in the threads, so children must stay focused on the task.

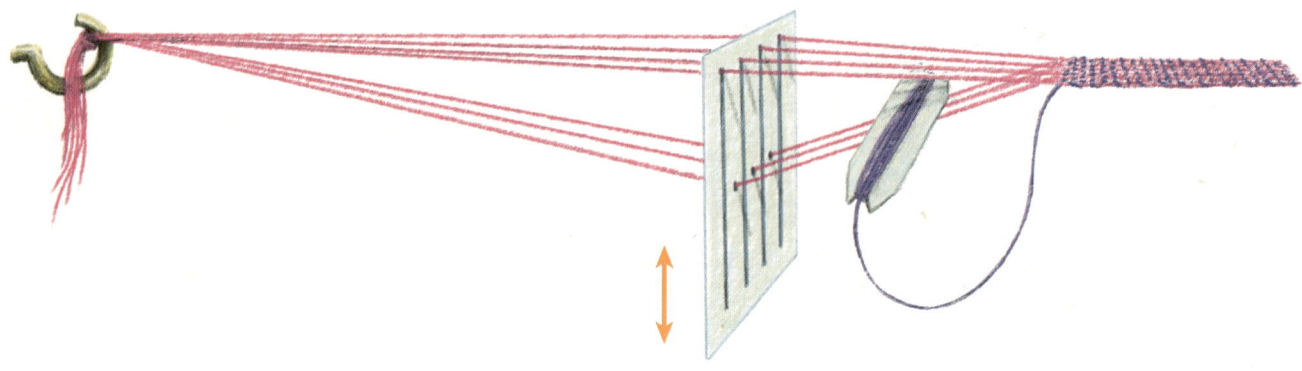

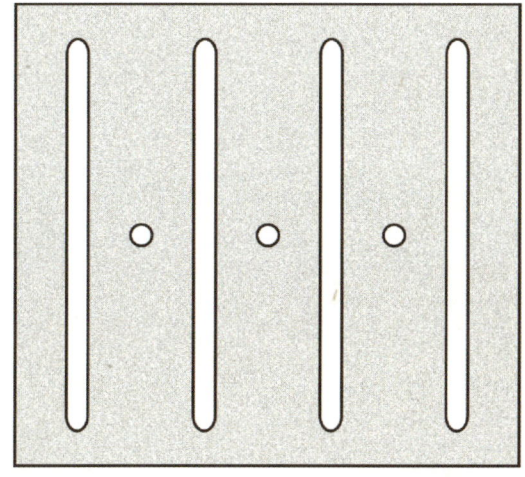

Young weavers demonstrate their skills on a loom at a craft market.

Weaving on a table-top loom.

Weaving with the weaving card is good preperation for working with the floor loom.

KNITTING

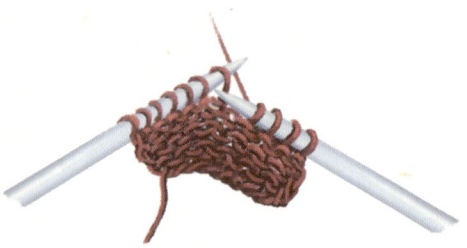

The farmer goes through

the gate,

pulls out a sheep

and closes the gate again.

From the age of about six, children enjoy learning to knit as long as they have enough dexterity. Thick needles, preferably made from sticks, are best, as well as strong yarn, hand-spun where possible.

To make knitting needles, take sticks that are about ¼ inch (5–7 mm) thick and about 8 inches (20 cm) long. Twigs from hazel bushes work well. Sharpen them at one end with a pencil sharpener, then sand them until smooth. Glue a wooden bead or piece of cork to the other end to prevent the stitches from slipping off.

To make it easier to get started, and to make the knitting more stable, an adult can knit the first few rows.

Knitted cloth can be used to make many objects, including soft toys. Experience shows that animals made with the children are especially well cared for.

FELTING

Making felt from carded wool is one of the oldest known textile techniques. Making dry felt from sheep's wool is fun for even the youngest children, but only small objects should be made with children – balls, beads and friendship bracelets – because these things can be finished fairly quickly. Larger pieces require more patience and are better for adults.

Making felt balls

Make a small, tight core out of raw wool, and then wrap a layer of plain carded wool around the core. The carded layer must be carefully pulled apart, and should not be twisted. Add a final thin layer of coloured wool. The fibres should be smooth and loose, otherwise the wool will not stick together. The wool ball should be the right size to fit in a child's hand.

Roll the dry ball until the hair ends begin to hook into each other. Then wet the child's hands with soapsuds (1 tablespoon of soap to 1 litre or quart of water), so the ball can be turned between the palms of the hands. The child then wets and turns the ball alternately. The wool should not stick to the child's hands; if this happens, not enough soapsuds are being used.

To begin with, the ball should only be turned, not squeezed. After a while the soapsuds soak the entire ball, and when the outer layer has become more stable, more pressure can be applied. The soapsuds should be around 104–122 °F (40–50 °C), and the ball can start to be dipped into them occasionally. Keep working and don't become impatient. Making felt requires perseverance.

Place the wool balls onto a towel on a table and roll them until they are solid. This will produce a tight ball which should then be washed in clear, cold water.

Small felt balls attached to tight threads make wonderful necklaces and they go well with friendship bracelets in matching colours.

Friendship bracelets

To make a friendship bracelet, take a ribbon of carded wool about 12 inches (30 cm) long and about 3/8 inch (1 cm) thick when pressed, and roll it back and forth with wet hands in soapsuds. Form the wool into a tight sausage until no fibres can be pulled out, then knot the ends together to form a bracelet of the right size.

The initial wool ribbons can also be knotted or braided together before they are felted for different effects.

First attempts at making felt from raw wool in hot soapsuds.

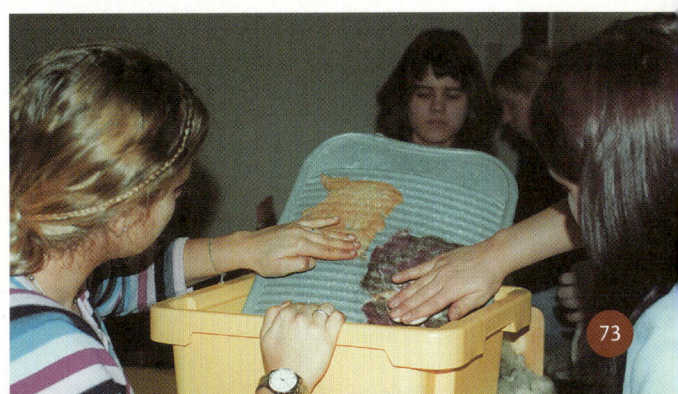

Free play with wool

There are many opportunities for free play in a wool workshop. Children often associate wool with snowflakes, and white wool can start to float through the air. Sometimes, children cover themselves from head to toe with wool fleece and pretend to hibernate, like plants under the snow. This way they experience the special warmth and quality of the wool.

Some children like to fall into the wool basket or a pile of wool fleece. They feel comfortable, safe and warm there. A six-year-old girl who, in freezing outdoor temperatures, was dressed in synthetic leggings, a cotton sweatshirt and thin socks told us after the first hour of work in the wool workshop that, for the first time in her life, she had warm hands.

Stories

Telling children fairy tales and stories which fit in with the projects they're doing can add a new dimension to their experience, by communicating on an emotional level. There are several Grimm's fairy tales suitable for use in a wool workshop:

- A Pack of Ragamuffins
- Rumpelstiltskin
- Mother Holle
- The Spindle, the Shuttle and the Needle
- The Three Spinners

Experience has shown that the children want to hear the fairy tales at least three times, and preferably more; it helps them to better connect with the mood of the story.

MAGIC WOOL

Wool that has been cleaned, finely carded and dyed is often called 'magic wool' or 'fairy wool'.

Before dyeing wool, make sure it's completely clean. After that, the procedure for dyeing wool is the same as for dyeing silk or cotton. (A description of dyeing cloth can be found in the *Spring and Summer Nature Activities for Waldorf Kindergartens* book, along with a chart of plant dye colours.) With wool, however, you need to work at higher temperatures, and allow a longer time for steeping and dyeing. Wool that has not yet been carded can also be dyed, and it can be fun to let children experiment.

Plant dyes are harder to come by in winter but in an emergency, they can be purchased from craft supply shops; alternatively, try a dye bath made from onion skins.

After steeping, rinsing, dyeing and drying the wool, card it enough that it becomes soft and fluffy, earning it the name 'fairy wool'. It now has many uses:

- ✪ Young children like to just look at it and feel it.
- ✪ It can be used to create colourful wool pictures or wall hangings, on a background of felt or burlap. This kind of activity is an ideal cross-generational project.
- ✪ It can be used to make felt, as described on p.73.
- ✪ Various human and animal shapes can be made from it, with or without a 'skeleton', to cuddle and play with in a doll's house or farm, or to make puppets for plays.

There are lots of things to make with magic wool, and there are some excellent books on the subject (see Resources at the end of the book).

Simple wool dolls made from magic wool.

These figures made from unspun dyed sheep's wool are for a puppet play.

FEBRUARY

1. To begin constructing a latticework willow hedge, dig a ditch as deep as possible.

2. Trim the small twigs off selected willow branches, which should be 6.5 ft (2 m) long and 2 inches (5 cm) in diameter, and as straight as possible.

3. Lay the willow branches in a diagonal grid at the desired intervals. Strip the bark from the branches where they cross each other.

4. Secure these crossing points with screws.

WILLOW HEDGE

Willow is a good plant for children to work with because it grows so fast, and is soft and flexible. Willows take root in the ground almost visibly: fill a large jar with sand, pebbles and water, stick a willow branch in, and watch the roots grow.

February is a good time to work with willow as long as the ground is no longer frozen and is not too wet. Some countries don't allow you to cut willow after March 1, to protect the catkins for bees, so plan well. There are also willow projects in the *Spring and Summer Nature Activities for Waldorf Kindergartens* book. Here are instructions for making a lattice-work willow hedge.

Willow hedges used as living fences are a good way to divide outdoor areas into play spaces and rest spaces for children. This hedge was built near a beehive to keep bees away from a nearby road and to provide food (catkins) and shelter (leaves).

5. Carefully cut a long strip of bark from the ends of the branches that will be put into the ditch. This will enable the branches to absorb water better.

6. Put the bound branch structure into the ditch and water well before the ditch has been filled with earth, so that the cuttings will get a good start in developing their roots.

Children's rooms today are often filled with objects with which the children have no real relationship. Modern mass-produced toys can stifle children's imagination, do nothing to satisfy a child's desire for real-life experiences, and present a distorted image of the world and human beings. How can we even start to tackle these problems?

The important thing is to *start*. We need to pass on a love of wood and natural materials to our children, and this shouldn't be hard: the relationship between people and nature is already strong. Collect a small supply of wood when you're out and about, and inspire children with what they can learn, and what can be made, from wood.

Children feel a deep relationship with toys that have been made in their presence and with their help. The toys will be handled carefully and treasured much more than anonymous mass-produced toys. In addition, working with wood stimulates children's imagination and helps them to gain fine motor skills.

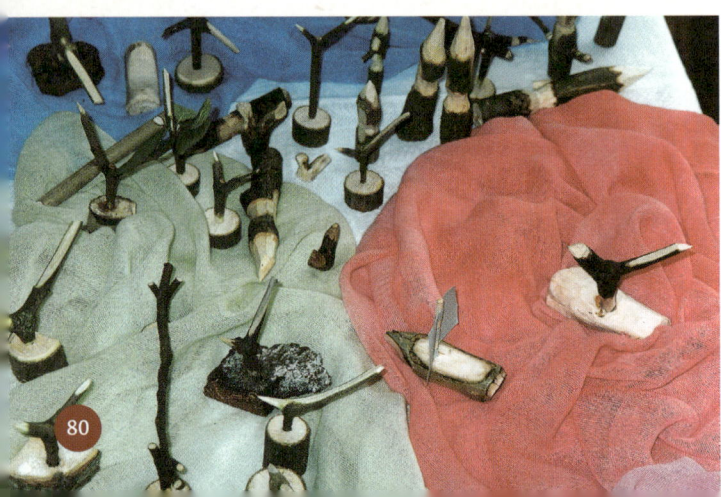

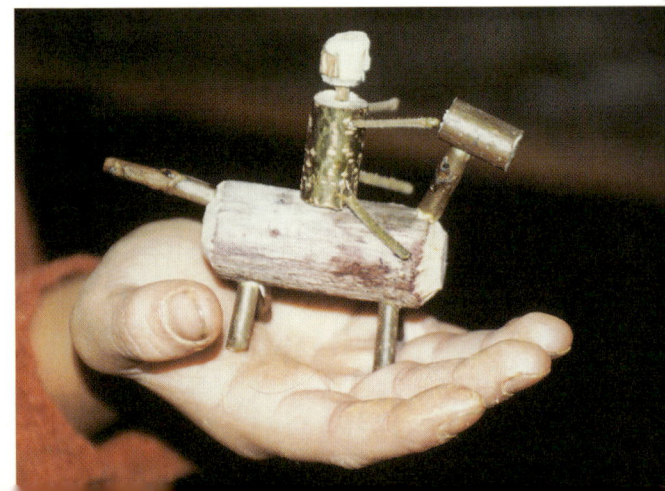

WOODEN TOYS

Wood is a sustainable, living material with infinite uses. Working with wood is very special: even after being shaped, it still has life. For any piece of wood, we must work to understand its hardness, weight and flexibility.

Wood should be cut before spring arrives and the saps begin to rise. The winter frost 'freeze-dries' the wood, making it easier to move and process.

coping saw

stick chisel

mitre saw

angular hollow chisel

foxtail saw

lopping shears

bow saw

carving knife

screw awl

mitre box

wood or leather mallet

rasp or file

brace and bit

hand drill

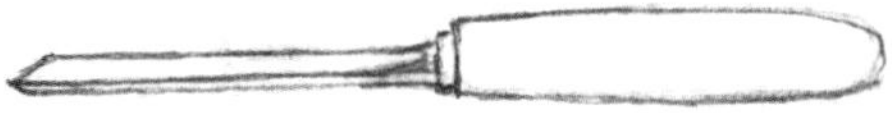

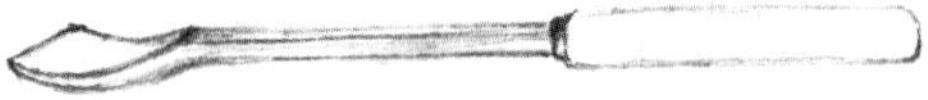

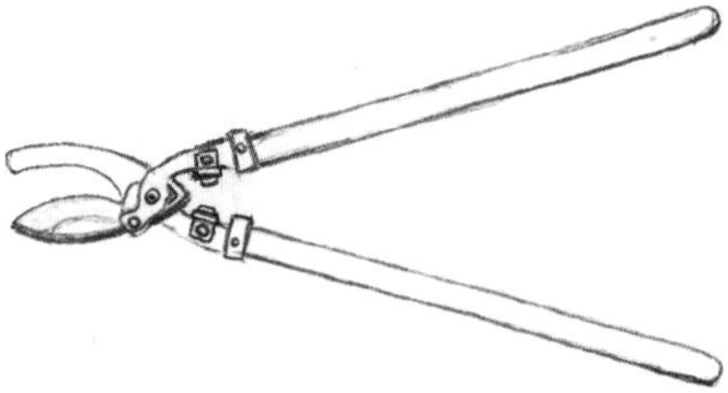

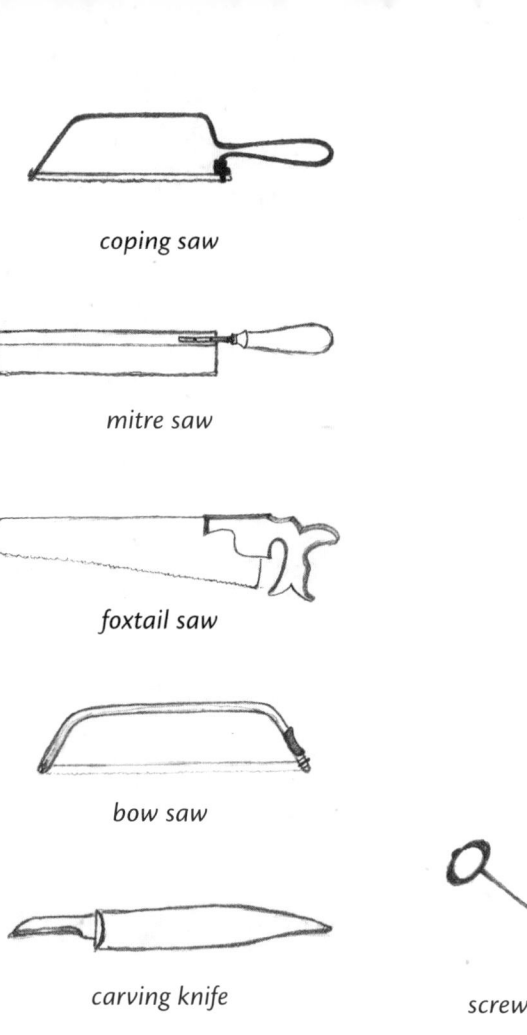

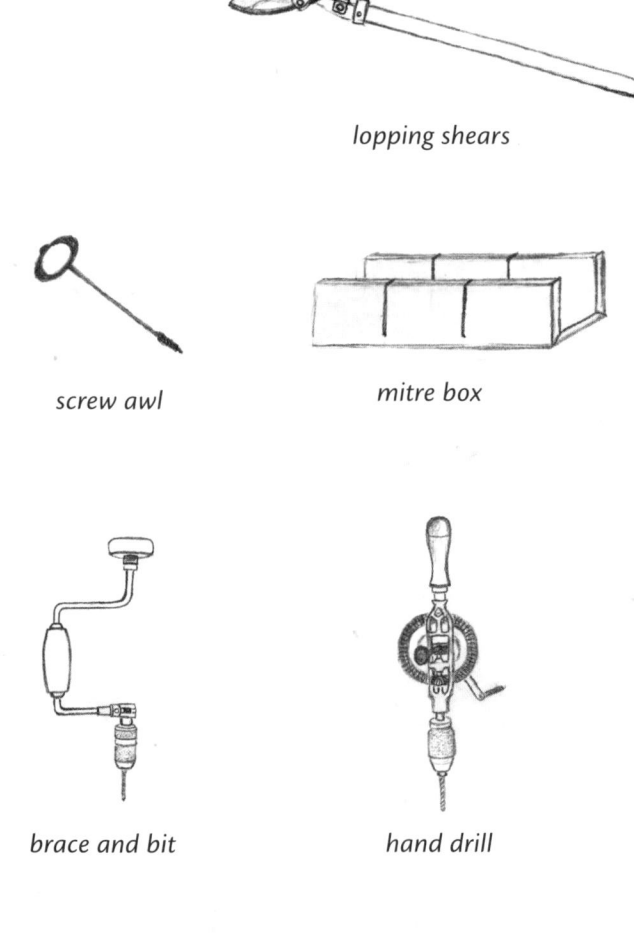

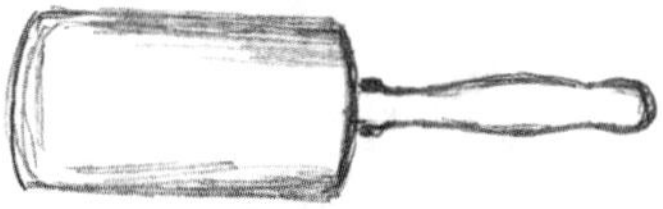

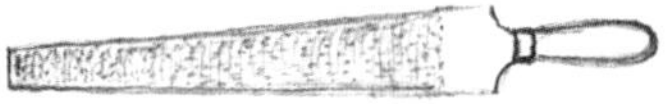

Tools

Kindergarten children should experience the physical qualities of wood directly, with their own hands and bodies.

Tools suitable for slightly older kindergarten children (age six or seven) include rough and fine saws, hand drills, hammers, pliers, screwdrivers, files and mitre boxes. A variety of clamps can be useful as well. For adults or school-age children (seven and older), other tools can be available, such as awls for making holes, chisels, carving knives, mallets and garden shears.

Tools, either purchased or hand-made, have their own value and should be treated with care. Drawing an outline of each tool on the wall where it hangs will help keep things in their rightful places.

At the beginning of each workshop, place the tools into a neat circle, name them while placing them, and then play a game. One child leaves the room; a tool is removed or placed in another spot and the child must then try to guess what has changed (top).

A mix of purchased and hand-made tools: mallets, awls, chisels and files (middle).

Tool wall in a Waldorf kindergarten (bottom).

Toy fences

Once children have mastered some basic tools, they can move on to creating all kinds of fences and railings for a toy farm or zoo.

Fences which aren't glued are a wonderful woodwork poject for children. They can be changed and moved continously, stretching a child's dexterity and imagination.

- ✪ Use round pieces of wood, forked branches, or pieces of dowling, and saw them to size.
- ✪ If necessary, split the round pieces of wood length-ways with a kitchen knife and a small hammer.
- ✪ Drill holes for the joints using a hand drill or a spiral drill.
- ✪ Sand all the individual pieces until they're beautifully smooth.
- ✪ Treat all the finished pieces with a natural oil: linseed oil or beeswax work well.

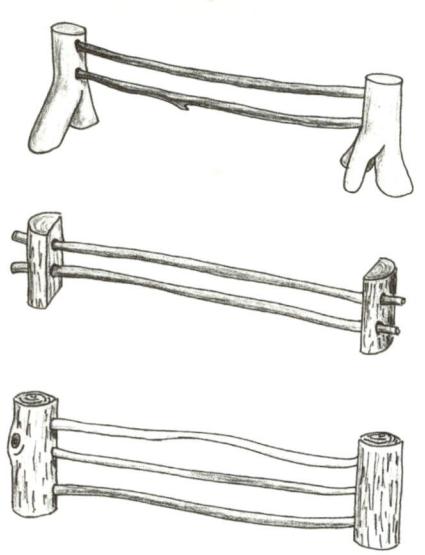

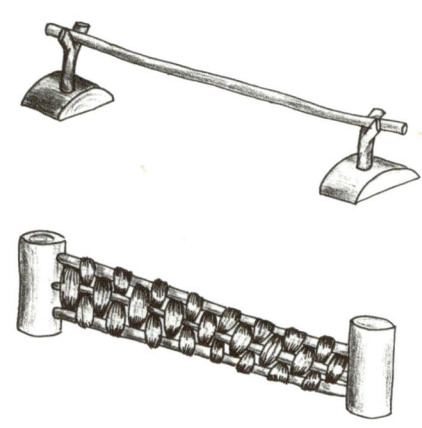

Toy furniture

Children often enjoy making miniature furniture for a hand-made doll's house from knotted branches.

- ✪ To make a chair, saw a branch on a diagonal (a small saw is best for this) then carve out a hollow for sitting and sand it well.
- ✪ A table or stool can be made from a section of a branch that has been finely sanded and sealed or waxed.
- ✪ When making a bench, carve the base flat so that the bench will sit straight. Then saw the seat and arms at the correct angle, along the length of the grain.
- ✪ Each piece should be finely sanded, so that it feels good in the child's hand.

The walls of these doll houses are made of plywood. They can be adjusted into different arrangements of rooms and easily folded together after playing. The furniture is carved from knotted branches; this activity is best done with an adult helping.

CARVING TWIGS IN KINDERGARTEN

This is an account of a twig-carving workshop in a local kindergarten.

The children gathered in the kindergarten playground, and the kindergarten teacher said: "All children who will be starting school next year, get a chair. Today, we're going to carve something together."

A circle of chairs quickly formed. In the middle, the teacher spread out a colourful cloth and placed various tools on it: simple knives and kitchen knives with wooden handles in a box, garden shears, small hand drills, sandpaper, and a box on which a red cross was painted.

"Now children," said the teacher, "place your hands on your hips and sit far enough apart so that you don't touch your neighbour, because for carving you need a lot of room. Now hold your hands in front of you and move your fingers. Who can wiggle them really fast? What do you see here? The best tools of all are your hands. With them you can do almost anything. Even better, you always have them with you!

"For some jobs, however, we need simple tools such as a knife for carving, a drill for drilling, or saws for sawing. We can't perform these jobs with our own fingers, but tools will help us. They are here on the cloth, sorted into groups. Look at them carefully. Now close your eyes. Now open your eyes. What has changed? That's right, one of the saws is now between the drills. Well done!

"Each of you take a knife out of the box when I come around. Remember that they are sharp so be careful. Let's look at the knives. They have a wooden handle, like the knives in your kitchen, and a blade. The blade has two edges. One edge is wider and you can run your finger carefully over that edge; that is the back of the knife. The other edge is the cutting edge; never run your fingers over that edge, because it is very sharp. When working, always hold only the handle and always carve toward the middle of the circle of chairs, never towards your neighbour.

"If you are not carving and want to stand up, lay the knife on your chair. Never walk around with the

knife in your hand! If you remember all of these important rules, we might not need the sticking plasters from the box with the red cross.

"I've collected some branches and twigs in the garden and woods. Tomorrow we'll do this together, but we must never break off fresh branches, because then the trees and bushes will cry.

"In this branch here, with a lot of knots, little birds are hiding, with a tiny head, a tail, and tiny legs. We want to look for them. Who has discovered one?"

The teacher points to a little girl.

"This is the tail, that's the head with the beak, and here are the legs. This bird is singing and chirping," says the little girl.

"Very good," says the teacher. "Now you." She points to a little boy.

"There's the head with the beak; here is the tail, and those are the legs. It has just discovered a seed on the ground and is picking it up," says the little boy.

"Excellent," says the teacher. "Now we'll take the garden shears and cut off all the wood that doesn't fit the little birds we've found. I'll help you if it's hard. For now, we'll leave the legs as they are. On the head we'll carve a sharp beak and make the tail thinner above and below, so that the bird is lighter and can fly better.

"At the moment, we can only hold the bird in our hands or lay it down, but birds need to be able to stand on their legs when they sing and pick up seeds. We'll saw a round disc from an elderberry branch, because this piece of wood already has a hole in it. Can you see the hole? Smooth the disc well with sandpaper. Now, hold the bird by its legs, think up a magic saying, and stick the legs into the natural hole in the wooden disc. If soft pith shows at the bottom, you can take that out. Now we know how big the legs have to be. If the legs are too thick, carve them to be thinner; if they are too thin, we can use a piece of wood as a wedge. Later on you can use chestnuts, beeswax, or clay as a stand.

Now, go to work!"

↑ This graceful water castle, created from hard root wood, is a natural work of art with great play value in the sandbox.

↑ A roof tile is prepared with a draw knife on the clamp bench.

↓ Making owl houses out of tree trunks with rotten cores.

↓ Children have worked very hard on this piece of fir with a rotten core, to keep the natural beauty of the branches inside intact.

MORE WOOD PROJECTS

↑ A clamp bench with an attached sawhorse; the wood is prepared here and then turned on a lathe.

↓ Branches of different thicknesses were joined together to make these simple forms – and the children couldn't be happier playing on the backs of them.

↑ If you want to become an expert, you must start practising early...

↓ ...and it takes a lot of practice to hit a nail on the head.

When dividing the clay into portions, keep in mind the size of the children's hands. They should be able to surround the portion with both hands.

Many hands are involved in building a table-top landscape from clay.

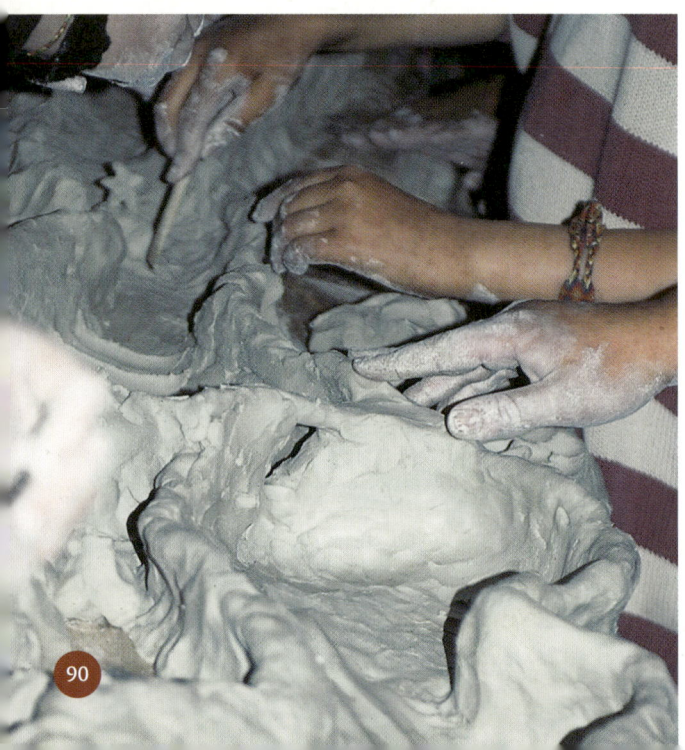

Pottery with children

- ✪ Creating objects from clay is relatively time-consuming due to the necessary drying and firing time. For this reason, begin the work early.
- ✪ For every clay object, cut a round disc from cardboard and place under the clay; this prevents the clay from sticking to the table while it is being shaped or dried.
- ✪ Make clay available as often as possible and in large quantities in tubs or, better yet, as a pile. Children should not work too long with clay in cooler weather, because it extracts too much warmth from their hands.
- ✪ Small amounts of clay can be formed into balls, packed in wet cloths or foil, and placed on the radiator for several hours before beginning work; the clay will then not be so cold.
- ✪ Fire simple clay objects as follows:
  - ✪ Place the objects into the kiln
  - ✪ Slowly heat the kiln to 1740 °F (950 °C)
  - ✪ Continue the firing
  - ✪ Slowly heat the kiln to 2190 °F (1200 °C)
- ✪ For more on making a clay oven, see *Spring and Summer Nature Activities for Waldorf Kindergartens*.

WORKING WITH CLAY

Creating things with clay is a basic craft activity which is good for all children to do, especially those with particular behavioural or psychological needs.

Making pottery has been part of human history for almost as long as we know. Archaeologists have discovered clay objects all over the world, many made using the same techniques as we use today: that is, by hand.

Through touching and moulding clay with their hands, children learn about key concepts such as smooth and rough, damp and dry, inside and outside. Clay has a good mix of characteristics which can lead to focused, contented activity, even in normally restless children.

In February, outdoor play can still be limited by bad weather and darkness, so working with clay gives children an activity involving a natural, outdoor material that can be carried out indoors: the perfect combination for this time of year.

Clay activities are suitable and popular all year round.

Sowing wheat seeds in earth-filled clay bowls.

Bowls for spouting grain

Spring is coming, and clay bowls and pots are needed to plant flowers and grain in March.

Use a lump of clay about the size of a large apple (keeping in mind the size of the child's hands). Make a nice smooth ball, and it place it on a cardboard disc. It's good to start by teaching a pinch pot technique: the right thumb presses a hollow into the ball, while the left hand presses against the ball. This way the child can feel, and alter, the thickness of the bowl. In fact, pressure from the inside and outside along with rhythmical turning is the secret to making all round vessels. If the outer surface splits, it can be smoothed over with wet fingers or a knife or spatula.

When the bowls have dried a bit, tap the bottoms carefully upwards to make them flat, so that the finished bowl won't wobble. Place them onto newspaper or cardboard in a space protected from drafts and extreme temperature changes, and leave to dry for seven to fourteen days, depending on the thickness of the bowls. In this raw state, the bowls are very fragile and can break easily, so they need to be handled as carefully as eggs.

Finally, fire the bowls. The high temperatures make the bowls so hard that they let almost no moisture through, so it's not necessary to glaze them. This is known as sintering.

Insects and birds

As a natural material, clay is very well suited to making nesting boxes for solitary insects such as hermit bees, bumblebees and wasps who naturally live in old wood. Drill holes between 1/8 and 3/8 inches wide (3 and 10 mm) into clay nests, drilling as deeply as possible. The insects will use them during the warm season.

Bird baths can also be made from clay. It is important to keep the edges low, and to build up a small mound in the middle so the birds can use it for both bathing and drinking. Use a firing temperature of 2190 °F (1200 °C) to make the bird bath partially frost-resistant. Children will enjoy filling the bird bath with fresh water, and this is a good opportunity to teach small children that our protection of nature depends on reliable, continuous care. It's never too early for children to learn this.

Making a bird bath can be communal activity.

Nests for solitary insects such as hermit bees, bumblebees and wasps.

RESOURCES

Suppliers

The following websites provide resources for crafting and more.

Australia

Morning Star
www.morningstarcrafts.com.au

North America

Bella Luna Toys
www.bellalunatoys.com

Ravelry wool store
www.ravelry.com

The Waldorf Shop
www.waldorfshop.net

UK

Conscious Craft
www.consciouscraft.uk

Myriad Natural Toys
www.myriadonline.co.uk

Waldorf Schools

There are currently over 1,100 Waldorf schools and nearly 2,000 Early Years settings in over 60 countries around the world. The following organisations can provide up-to-date information.

World

International Association for Steiner Waldorf Early Childhood Education
www.iaswece.or

Australia

Steiner Education Australia
www.steinereducation.edu.au

New Zealand

Steiner Education Aotearoa New Zealand
www.seanz.org

North America

Association of Waldorf Schools of North America
www.waldorfeducation.org

South Africa

Southern African Federation of Waldorf Schools
www.waldorf.org.za

UK

Steiner Waldorf Schools Fellowship
www.steinerwaldorf.org

Spring and Summer Nature Activities for Waldorf Kindergartens

Irmgard Kutsch and Brigitte Walden

'This is a wonderful resource book for Steiner-Waldorf kindergartens! It is full of ideas and projects for educators on how to help children engage with the seasons.'
– *Kindling*

Encourage children to engage with the seasons as they build bird boxes, use plant dyes, make earthworm boxes, grow and cook fresh herbs, create Easter bowls and care for butterflies.

As well as fun nature activities – both indoor and outside – for children, this book also includes valuable background reading and advice for teachers, such as how to create your own kindergarten garden.

florisbooks.co.uk

More craft and activity books to enjoy with children

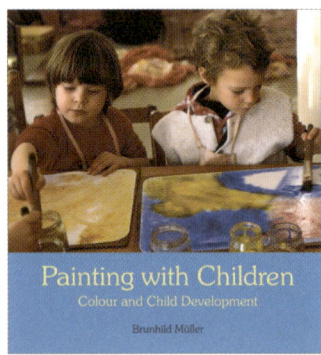
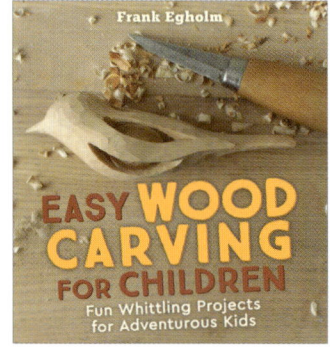
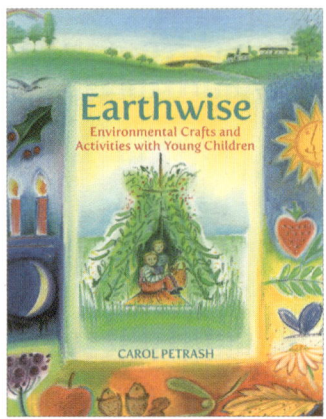

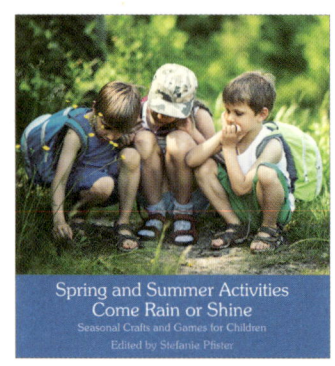

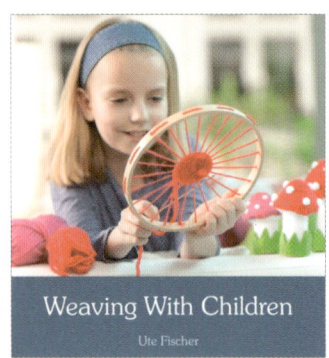
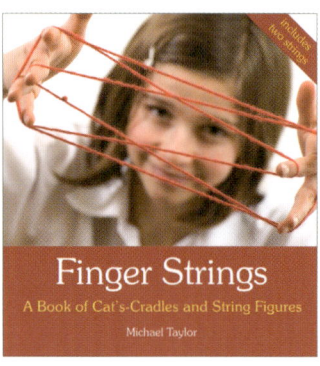

 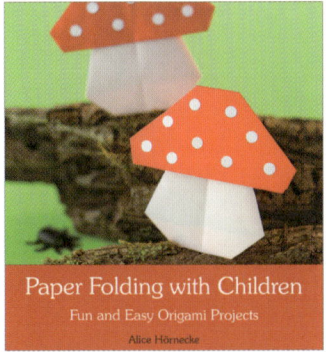 

  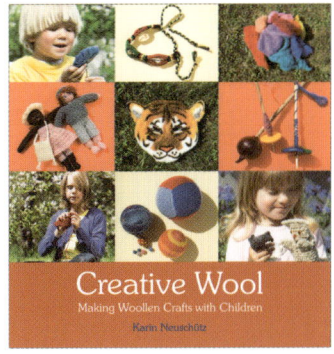

For news on all the latest books, and to get exclusive discounts, join our mailing list at:

florisbooks.co.uk/signup

And get a FREE book with every online order!

We will never pass your details to anyone else.